INSIDE PROFESSIONAL SOCCER
FC BAYERN MUNICH
Heather Williams
MEDIA ENHANCED BOOKS
AV2 BY WEIGL
ADDED VALUE • AUDIO VISUAL
www.av2books.com

Go to www.av2books.com, and enter this book's unique code.

BOOK CODE

AVU66537

AV² by Weigl brings you media enhanced books that support active learning.

AV² provides enriched content that supplements and complements this book. Weigl's AV² books strive to create inspired learning and engage young minds in a total learning experience.

Your AV² Media Enhanced books come alive with...

Audio
Listen to sections of the book read aloud.

Key Words
Study vocabulary, and complete a matching word activity.

Video
Watch informative video clips.

Quizzes
Test your knowledge.

Embedded Weblinks
Gain additional information for research.

Slide Show
View images and captions, and prepare a presentation.

Try This!
Complete activities and hands-on experiments.

... and much, much more!

Published by AV² by Weigl
350 5th Avenue, 59th Floor
New York, NY 10118
Website: www.av2books.com

Library of Congress Control Number: 2018930414

ISBN 978-1-4896-7787-7 (hardcover)
ISBN 978-1-4896-7788-4 (softcover)
ISBN 978-1-4896-7789-1 (multi-user eBook)

Printed in the United States of America in Brainerd, Minnesota
1 2 3 4 5 6 7 8 9 0 22 21 20 19 18

022018
120817

Project Coordinator: John Willis   Designer: Terry Paulhus

The publisher acknowledges Getty Images and Alamy as its primary image suppliers for this title.

CONTENTS

Introduction

Munich is the third-largest city in Germany. It is known for BMW cars and hosting the world-famous Oktoberfest. It is also home to one of professional soccer's best-known teams, Bayern Munich.

Football Club (FC) Bayern Munich is a German sports organization. The club includes basketball, handball, table tennis, and chess. However, Bayern is best known for its very successful soccer team. In most European countries, soccer is known as football.

Colombian midfielder James Rodriguez started taking German lessons when he transferred to Bayern Munich in 2017.

Bayern has been around for more than 100 years. It has survived two world wars and many coaching changes. Bayern is part of the **Bundesliga**, Germany's top soccer league. Some of the world's most successful coaches and talented athletes have worn Bayern's colors.

Robert Lewandowski has helped Bayern win several championships with his quick goal-scoring abilities.

FC BAYERN MUNICH

Arena Allianz Arena

Division Bundesliga

Head Coach Jupp Heynckes

Location Munich, Bavaria (Bayern), Germany

FIFA Club World Cups 1

Nicknames *Die Bayern* ("The Bavarians"), *Die Roten* ("The Reds"), FC Hollywood

11 Trophies won by Klaus Augenthaler

2 Intercontinental Cups

17 Bundesliga opponents

6 German Super Cups

2,874 Foil panels on the Allianz Arena

History

Bayern's 1965 German Cup win was the beginning of a very successful decade for the team, often called "The Golden Years."

In 1900, Franz John and 16 others decided to form a soccer team. They called the club *Fußball-Club Bayern München*, or "FC Bayern Munich." However, they needed money and a place to play. They joined a sports organization called Münchner Sportclub (MSC) in 1906. MSC provided the team with white shirts and red shorts. Bayern's earliest nickname was *Die Rothosen*, or "The Red Shorts." Bayern won its first regional championship in 1926 and its first national **title** in 1932.

Bayern lost its coach, several players, and its home **pitch** during World War II. When the Bundesliga **division** was formed in 1963, Bayern was not chosen to join. Two years later, in 1965, with the help of legendary players Sepp Maier, Gerd Müller, and Franz Beckenbauer, Bayern was promoted to the Bundesliga division. Bayern went on to dominate the Bundesliga until 1979.

The next 20 years were filled with ups and downs for Bayern. The team faced many coaching changes during the 1980s and 1990s. The team was still able to stay competitive. They won several Bundesliga championships during these decades, and even a UEFA Cup in 1996. From 2000 to the present, the team has experienced one of its most successful periods. In 2013, Bayern won the FIFA Club World Cup for the first time.

Top goal scorer Gerd Müller led Bayern to three European Cups from 1973 to 1976.

The Arena

Austrian **mountaineers** mounted the light panels on Allianz Arena. Some of these were up to **82 feet** (25 meters) off the ground.

Allianz Arena's foil panels are constantly inflated by thousands of small fans built into the stadium walls.

For its first few decades, Bayern played matches in a Munich park called Leopoldstraße (LEH-oh-pohld-strahss-uh). In 1925, they moved to Grünwalder Stadion. Bayern shared Grünwalder with 1860 Munich, a rival team, until the 1970s. Both teams moved to the Olympiastadion in 1972 and remained there until the early 2000s.

Allianz Arena was completed in 2005. It is one of Europe's most unique stadiums. The exterior is made up of almost 3,000 inflatable foil panels. There are more than 300,000 lights behind the panels. At night, the stadium glows brightly. It is lit red for Bayern home matches and white for German national team matches. It can turn many other colors as well, depending on the evening's event. Allianz Arena can seat up to 75,000 people.

Until recently, Allianz Arena was home pitch to both Bayern and 1860 Munich. In 2017, 1860 Munich moved and Bayern became the sole club team to call the stadium its home. Bayern shares the space with the German national team. In addition, several 2006 FIFA World Cup games were played there.

Allianz Arena was the first stadium in the world that could completely change colors.

Where They Play

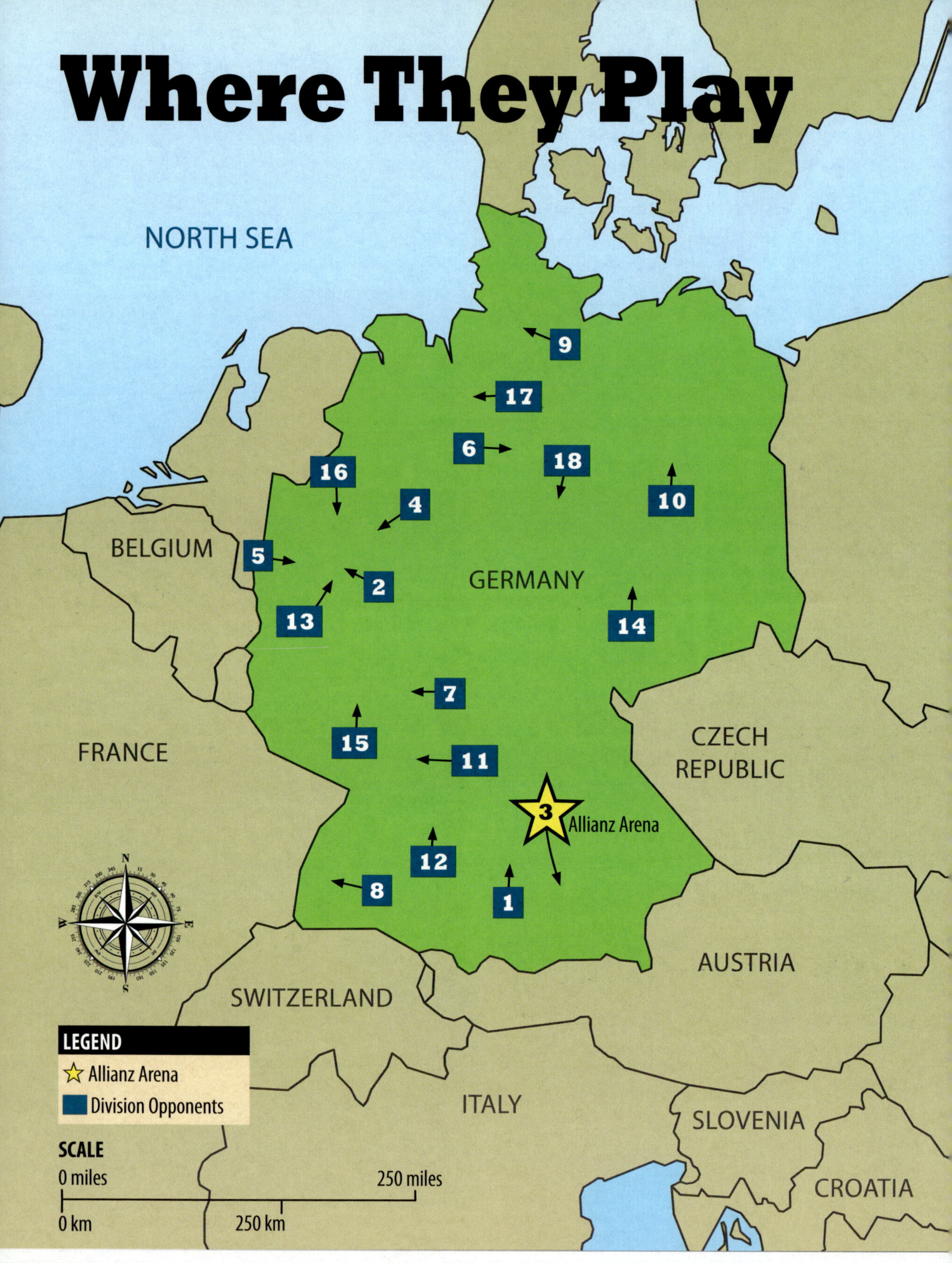

Arena
Allianz Arena

Location
Munich, Germany

Broke Ground
October 2002

Completed
May 2005

Field Design
The stadium is a rectangular structure with covered seating, an open-air playing field, and retractable roller blinds to block the Sun.

Features
- *FCB Erlebniswelt*, meaning "The Inner World of FCB," is a museum in the stadium devoted to the history of FC Bayern
- Nicknamed *Schlauchboot*, which means "inflatable boat"
- 10,400 seats convert to a standing area for extra space

BUNDESLIGA TEAMS

1 FC Augsburg *(Augsburg, Germany)*
2 Bayer 04 Leverkusen *(Leverkusen, Germany)*
★3 Bayern Munich *(Munich, Germany)*
4 Borussia Dortmund *(Dortmund, Germany)*
5 Borussia Mönchengladbach *(Mönchengladbach, Germany)*
6 Hannover 96 *(Hannover, Germany)*
7 Eintracht Frankfurt *(Frankfurt, Germany)*
8 SC Freiburg *(Freiburg im Breisgau, Germany)*
9 Hamburger SV *(Hamburg, Germany)*
10 Hertha BSC *(Berlin, Germany)*
11 TSG 1899 Hoffenheim *(Sinsheim, Germany)*
12 VfB Stuttgart *(Stuttgart, Germany)*
13 1.FC Köln *(Cologne, Germany)*
14 RB Leipzig *(Leipzig, Germany)*
15 1. FSV Mainz 05 *(Mainz, Germany)*
16 FC Schalke 04 *(Gelsenkirchen, Germany)*
17 SV Werder Bremen *(Bremen, Germany)*
18 VfL Wolfsburg *(Wolfsburg, Germany)*

The Uniforms

Red was first introduced to the uniform when Bayern merged with another team, Munchner SC, in 1906.

HOME

The original Bayern **kit** colors were white and blue. During the club's early years, the kit colors switched to white and maroon. After joining the Bundesliga, the home colors shifted to blue and red, and eventually to just red. The home kits sometimes have white or blue accents. Away kits usually range from dark navy blue to black. There has also been the occasional light blue shirt, full turquoise kit, and even a yellow and green "Brazil" kit.

AWAY

The Bayern logo began as a simple blue and white flag. After one year, it was replaced by a green, gold, and red octagon. Today, the logo has evolved into a round seal with the team's name in an outer red circle. Inside the red circle is a smaller circle with a Bavarian flag background.

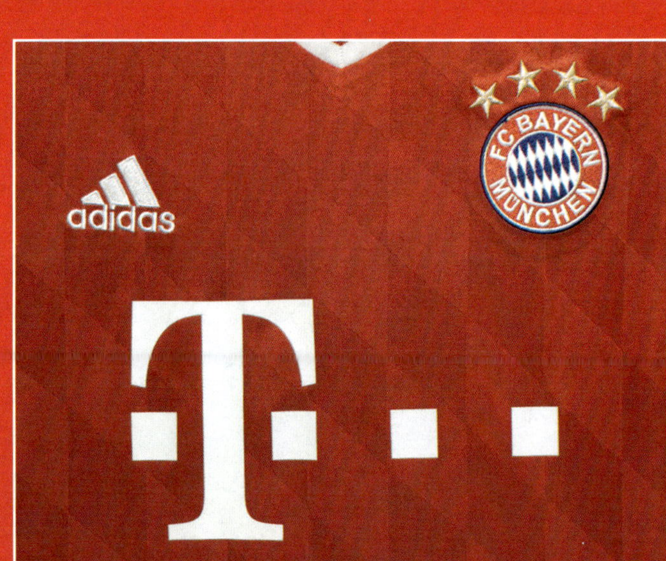

Its sponsors have changed over the years, but Bayern's team logo has not changed much since the 1966-1967 season.

Goalie Gear

The goalie is allowed to pick up the ball on the field as long as he remains inside the penalty box.

Goalkeepers must stand out from field players and field officials. Goalies usually wear long sleeves and often choose brightly colored jerseys. Bayern goalies often wear bright green or bright blue. They can wear pants, rather than shorts, if they choose. Most wear special goalkeeping gloves. These gloves have rubbery surfaces to help them grip the ball. Some goalkeeper gloves contain plastic spines to protect keepers' hands from injuries.

Bayern goalie and team captain Manuel Neuer is considered one of the best goalkeepers in the world. He has been described as a "sweeper keeper," because he often leaves the penalty box to clear the ball. Neuer is known for his quick reflexes, physical strength, and excellent field leadership. He often wears a black, navy blue, or lime green kit in the goal.

Manuel Neuer has been playing with Bayern since 2011.

The Coaches

Jupp Heynckes has been Bayern's head coach four different times in the team's history.

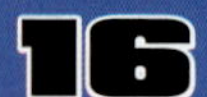

Bayern has had many coaches, but only those who have joined since the team became part of Bundesliga are considered official. The team has had 21 different coaches since 1963. Some of them served multiple times, so there have been 28 coaching changes between 1963 and 2017.

JUPP HEYNCKES Jupp Heynckes is Bayern's current coach. Heynckes has coached more than 300 matches with Bayern, and has won 9 titles with the team. During emotional or stressful moments in games, his face turns bright red. This has earned him the nickname "Osram," after a German light bulb company.

OTTMAR HITZFELD Ottmar Hitzfeld is Bayern's second most successful coach. He was also the club's second longest serving coach. Under his leadership, the team was very successful in the late 1990s. Hitzfeld was nicknamed *Der General*, or "The General." He won 14 major titles as coach of Bayern.

UDO LATTEK Bayern's most successful coach of all time was Udo Lattek. Lattek has been head coach at Bayern twice. In total, he served as head coach for more than 3,000 days. Lattek coached Bayern to 10 major titles. He is one of only two coaches to win all three major European titles.

Fans Around the World

Bayern fans go to great lengths to support their team, from marching into the stadium chanting and carrying huge flags, to adorning themselves from head to toe in team gear.

Allianz Arena holds up to 75,000 people. At every home Bayern match, most of those seats are filled. Bayern boasts more than 4,000 fan clubs. These fans are spread all over Germany and the world. The team has several online message boards, as well as multiple Facebook pages, a YouTube channel, and a Twitter feed.

The most extreme Bayern fans are the **ultras**. The most well-known ultra groups are the *Südkurve '73*, "The South Bank '73," and the *Schickeria München*, "The Munich In-Crowd." The ultras have special seating areas at home matches. They are also well known for singing chants and special songs during games.

Fan Traditions

#1 Each year, on the second Saturday of Munich's traditional Oktoberfest, the entire team and staff of Bayern come to the festival dressed in traditional Bavarian *lederhosen*.

#2 One Bayern ultra group, Schickeria München, was awarded the Julius Hirsch Award for its commitment to fighting discrimination.

Legends of the Past

Many great players have suited up for FC Bayern Munich. A few of them have become icons of the team and the city it represents.

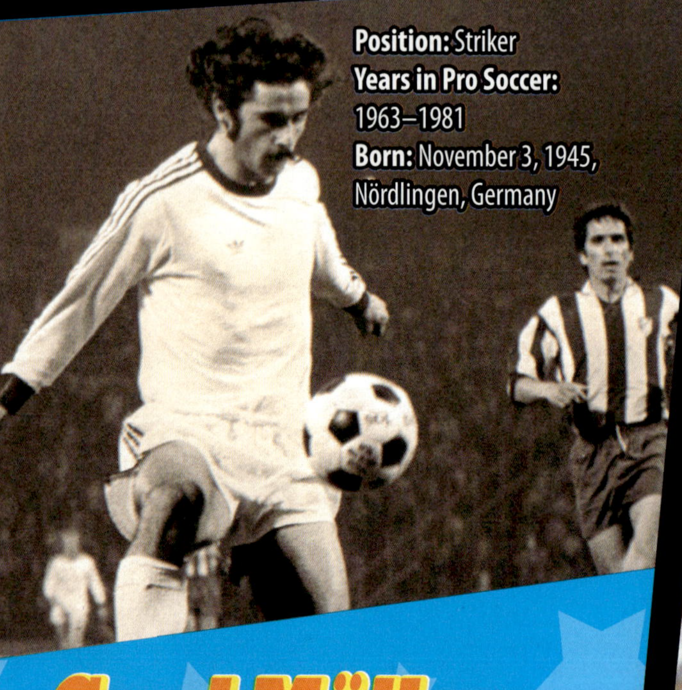

Position: Striker
Years in Pro Soccer: 1963–1981
Born: November 3, 1945, Nördlingen, Germany

Gerd Müller

Gerd Müller is one of the top goal scorers of all time. He was nicknamed *Der Bomber*, or "The Bomber." Müller was a member of the first Bayern team to be part of the Bundesliga. In his 15 seasons with Bayern, he scored 476 total goals in 541 matches. While playing for the West German national team, this talented **striker** averaged more than a goal per game. He was named German Footballer of the Year twice. Müller led Bayern to 14 titles.

Sepp Maier

Sepp Maier is considered one of the greatest German goalkeepers of all time. Meier spent his entire professional football career with Bayern. He made 600 total appearances as goalkeeper for Bayern, the most in the team's history. Meier also played for the West German national team in four FIFA World Cups. In 1974, he led West Germany to a World Cup championship. He was so quick that fans nicknamed him "The Cat From Anzing." Once, during a slow-paced Bayern match, Meier left the goal to chase a duck off the field.

Position: Goalkeeper
Years in Pro Soccer: 1962–1980
Born: February 28, 1944, Metten, Germany

Philipp Lahm

Philipp Lahm captained Bayern for six seasons. He led his team to eight Bundesliga titles. They also won the UEFA Champions League title, the UEFA Super Cup, and the FIFA Club World Cup during Lahm's time as captain. Despite being small, he was known for his precise tackles and speed. Lahm was a versatile **defender**, able to play many areas of the field. He made more than 500 appearances with Bayern and 113 with the German national team.

Position: Defender/Midfielder
Years in Pro Soccer: 2001–2017
Born: November 11, 1983, Munich, Germany

Lothar Matthäus

Lothar Matthäus was named World Footballer of the Year in 1991. Matthäus spent a total of 12 seasons with Bayern. He led the team back into a period of success, winning the division title seven times. Matthäus has 150 international appearances, or caps, more than any other German player in history. Matthäus also played in more World Cup games than any other player in history. He was considered a defensive player, but was also known for his strong shot. Matthäus scored 85 goals for Bayern and 23 for Germany.

Position: Midfielder/Defender
Years in Pro Soccer: 1979–2000
Born: March 21, 1961, Erlangen, Germany

Stars of Today

Today's FC Bayern Munich team is made up of many young, talented players who have proven that they are among the best in the league.

Thomas Müller

Forward Thomas Müller is one of Bayern's top scorers. He is well known for finding spaces in the opposing team's defense. Müller signed with the club in 2008 and is the team's co-captain. He has led Bayern to six Bundesliga titles, the UEFA Super Cup, and the FIFA Club World Cup. Müller is also a member of the German national team. He has scored more than 30 international goals for Germany and was part of the 2014 World Cup–winning team.

Position: Forward
Years in Pro Soccer: 2008–present
Born: September 13, 1989, Weilheim in Oberbayern, Germany

Arjen Robben

Arjen Robben joined Bayern in 2009. He has had a few injuries but is still a key member of the team. Robben scored the winning goal in the UEFA Champions League Final in 2013. He has helped Bayern reach the top of the Bundesliga six times. Robben is a versatile left-footed player. He is known to beat defenders to the ball quickly. Robben has scored more than half of his career goals with Bayern. He recently retired from the Netherlands national team with 96 appearances and 37 goals.

Position: Midfielder
Years in Pro Soccer: 2009–present
Born: January 23, 1984, Bedum, Netherlands

Franck Ribéry

Franck Ribéry has made more than 300 appearances with Bayern. Ribéry has been injured in almost every season he has played with Bayern. This has not stopped him from being a scoring threat for the team. Ribéry is a right-footed player who prefers playing on the left side of the field. This makes him an extremely versatile player. Ribéry is also the team joker and is known for playing pranks on teammates.

Position: Midfielder
Years in Pro Soccer: 2007–present
Born: April 7, 1983, Boulogne-sur-Mer, France

Robert Lewandowski

Robert Lewandowski is the captain for the Polish national team. He is also their all-time top goal scorer. In just over three seasons with Bayern, Lewandowski has scored more than 100 total goals. His per-game average is almost one goal per match. In the 2013–14 and 2015–16 seasons, Lewandowski was the Bundesliga top goal scorer. During the 2015–16 season, he scored five goals in just nine minutes against VfL Wolfsburg, setting a world record. Bayern has won the division title every season since Lewandowski joined the team.

Position: Striker
Years in Pro Soccer: 2014–present
Born: August 21, 1988, Warsaw, Poland

All-Time Records

27
Titles
Bayern has won the Bundesliga title a record 27 times.

5
Title Win Streak
Among all Bundesliga title winners, Bayern holds the record for the most consecutive wins, with five from 2013 to 2017.

53
Win Streak
From 2013 to 2014, Bayern won 53 consecutive games.

473

Games Played

Sepp Maier holds a record 473 total Bundesliga appearances with Bayern.

365

Goals Scored

Bayern's top Bundesliga division scorer of all time is Gerd Müller, with 365 goals.

Timeline

Throughout the team's history, FC Bayern Munich has had many memorable events that have become defining moments for the team and its fans.

1932
Bayern wins its first national title against Eintracht Frankfurt.

1900
Bayern is established as Fußball-Club Bayern München

1925
Bayern shares Grünwalder Stadion with rival club 1860 Munich.

1890 1900 1910 1920 1930 1940 1950

In 1910, Bayern joins Kreisliga, the first Bavarian football league.

1939
World War II leads to a suspension of club soccer. Bayern's coach is forced to leave the country.

The Future
In the past, when Bayern has failed, they have made coaching and roster changes to bring about success. The current team is made up of experienced players and young talent. Under the leadership of a winning coach, Bayern will no doubt continue to dominate the Bundesliga for years to come.

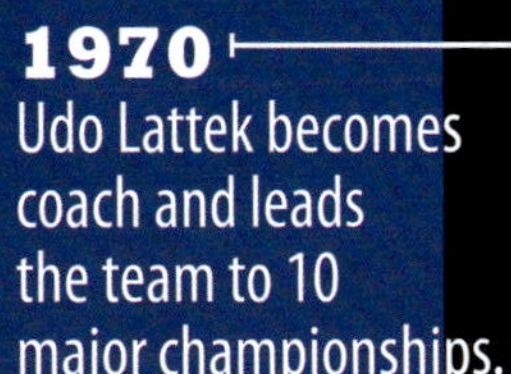

1970
Udo Lattek becomes coach and leads the team to 10 major championships.

2017
Jupp Heynckes is appointed coach for the fourth time in the club's history.

1960 1970 1980 1990 2000 2010 2020

In 1976, Bayern wins the European Cup Final for the third straight season.

1965
Bayern is promoted to the Bundesliga, where they have remained ever since.

1998
Ottmar Hitzfeld begins his six-year run as Bayern's second most successful coach and leads the team to a time of renewed success.

Write a Biography

Life Story

A person's life story can be the subject of a book. This kind of book is called a biography. Biographies often describe the lives of people who have achieved great success. These people may be alive today, or they may have lived many years ago. Reading a biography can help you learn more about a great person.

Get the Facts

Use this book, and research in the library and on the internet, to find out more about your favorite player. Learn as much about him as you can. What position does he play? What are his statistics in important categories? Has he set any records? Also, be sure to write down key events in the person's life. What was his childhood like? What has he accomplished off the field? Is there anything else that makes this person special or unusual?

Use the Concept Web

A concept web is a useful research tool. Read the questions in the concept web on the following page. Answer the questions in your notebook. Your answers will help you write a biography.

Concept Web

Adulthood
- Where does this individual currently reside?
- Does he or she have a family?

Your Opinion
- What did you learn from the books you read in your research?
- Would you suggest these books to others?
- Was anything missing from these books?

Childhood
- Where and when was this person born?
- Describe his or her parents, siblings, and friends.
- Did this person grow up in unusual circumstances?

Accomplishments off the Field
- What is this person's life's work?
- Has he or she received awards or recognition for accomplishments?
- How have this person's accomplishments served others?

Help and Obstacles
- Did this individual have a positive attitude?
- Did he or she receive help from others?
- Did this person have a mentor?
- Did this person face any hardships?
- If so, how were the hardships overcome?

Accomplishments on the Field
- What records does this person hold?
- What key games and plays have defined his career?
- What are his stats in categories important to his position?

Work and Preparation
- What was this person's education?
- What was his or her work experience?
- How does this person work?
- What is the process he or she uses?

Trivia Time

Take this quiz to test your knowledge of FC Bayern Munich. The answers are printed upside down under each question.

1 How many goals did Robert Lewandowski score in just nine minutes during a 2015 match?

A. Five

2 What year did Franz John and friends establish Bayern?

A. 1900

3 Allianz Arena turns what color for Bayern home matches?

A. Red

4 Who is Bayern's all-time top goal scorer?

A. Gerd Müller

5 How many times has Jupp Heynckes served as coach for Bayern?

A. Four

6 How many times has Bayern won the FIFA Club World Cup?

A. Once

7 Which legendary Bayern coach served for a total of more than 3,000 days?

A. Udo Lattek

8 What is Allianz Arena nicknamed due to its air-filled panels?

A. *Schlauchboot*, "The inflatable boat"

9 What is the meaning of *Die Roten*?

A. "The Reds"

Key Words

Bundesliga: the top professional club football league in Germany

defender: also called a back. A player who plays in front of the goal and stops the other team from scoring.

division: a group of teams who compete against each other for a championship

forward: a player on a soccer team who normally plays closest to the opponent's goal

goalkeepers: also called goalies. The players responsible for keeping the ball from going into the goal and the only players who are allowed to pick up the ball.

kit: the standard attire and equipment worn by soccer players, including a shirt, shorts, socks, and shin guards

pitch: an area that is used for playing sports

striker: a forward player who is the team's primary scorer

title: a championship

ultras: football fans known for extreme support of a football club

Index

Log on to www.av2books.com

AV² by Weigl brings you media enhanced books that support active learning. Go to www.av2books.com, and enter the special code found on page 2 of this book. You will gain access to enriched and enhanced content that supplements and complements this book. Content includes video, audio, weblinks, quizzes, a slide show, and activities.

AV² Online Navigation

Audio
Listen to sections of the book read aloud.

Book Pages
AV² pages directly correspond to pages in the book.

Video
Watch informative video clips.

Embedded Weblinks
Gain additional information for research.

Key Words
Study vocabulary, and complete a matching word activity.

Try This!
Complete activities and hands-on experiments.

Quizzes
Test your knowledge.

Slide Show
View images and captions, and prepare a presentation.

AV² was built to bridge the gap between print and digital. We encourage you to tell us what you like and what you want to see in the future.

Sign up to be an AV² Ambassador at www.av2books.com/ambassador.

Due to the dynamic nature of the Internet, some of the URLs and activities provided as part of AV² by Weigl may have changed or ceased to exist. AV² by Weigl accepts no responsibility for any such changes. All media enhanced books are regularly monitored to update addresses and sites in a timely manner. Contact AV² by Weigl at 1-866-649-3445 or av2books@weigl.com with any questions, comments, or feedback.